THANK YOU

for your order

Thank you for choosing this book to guide you on your journey. I appreciate your trust. And I hope that all the energy and the framework assistance that has been given here will be useful forever. I will always strive to provide the best according to your expectations. And I hope you love your order as much as I loved creating it!

I would love to see my books used by those who need them. Please tag me on your social media @annie.lightman

Ann Lightman

AweSoME PEOPLE GROUP

The information and suggestions given here are merely examples, and on their own merits have no bearing on your end results. They're only meant to help you in the right direction to develop your conversion skills. Therefore, feel free to customize, personalize what's given here and make your own effort to convert your leads and sky rocket your sales. I believe in you.

Ann Lightman

AweSoMe PEOPLE GROUP

HANDLING OOBJECTIONS FOR REAL ESTATE AGENTS

Handling objections is essential for growth and success in any industry and especially in the real estate market. Whether you're just starting as an agent or looking to expand your expertise, it's important to have a solid strategy in place. The framework in this book will help you create your own formula to overcome any objection, become a better communicator and achieve success in both your personal and professional life.

Be Uniquely You

01

The key to achieving anything is to learn and accept yourself. Begin with your wants and needs, and your professional goals. Gain clarity on who you want to serve and how.

Overcoming Objections

02

Understand the true nature of objections. Acknowledge and empathize with your customers perspective. Build stronger connections. And level-up to long-term success.

Practice Your Responses

03

You need to practice with intention and purpose, if you want to achieve excellence. This means setting specific goals, and seeking out constructive feedback from others.

Create Your Own Objection Handling Success Formula

04

Create your strategies and write down new responses that work. Remember to be flexible, your ability to adapt to new situations and embrace change can make all the difference in both your personal and professional life.

☎ 917-669-9259 | awesomepeoplegroup.com

BE YOU

Be uniquely you

One key to handling objections is having confidence. Confidence which comes from embracing what makes you unique. And, of course, your masterfully crafted skills, your support system and our exclusive energy and framework assistance given here, together will help you to do just that.

01

Ann Lightman

GET INSPIRED

1 —————————————————

UNDERSTAND
YOUR WORTH

2 —————————————————

VALUE YOUR
LIFE

3 —————————————————

APPRECIATE
YOUR BLESSINGS

THIS IS MY PLAN

Detailed strategy you will follow and use to guide
you and remind you of what you want to achieve.

I DO: INTERCEPT DIRECTION AND OPPORTUNITIES

TRANSFORM YOUR LIFE

The first step to transforming your life, is to transform your ideology and that begins with self acceptance. You simply cannot move forward with objections to your own success stemming from your own mindset. So before you could even begin to respond to your prospects' objections, you need to address your own.

Empower yourself with a transformative success plan. Start moving in the direction of a happy, more successful you!

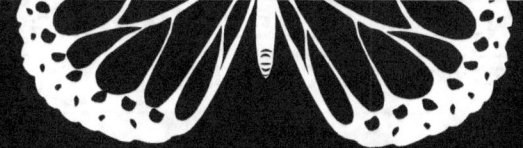

Selling doesn't have to be a daunting or uncomfortable endeavor. In fact, it can be enjoyable if you approach it in the right way. Start by focusing on building strong relationships with your customers. Remember to listen more than you speak, and keep in mind that there's a reason we have two ears and one mouth. Talk about your customers, not yourself, and don't be afraid to move on when it's time.

**MY BELIEFS AND CORE VALUES
WHEN IT COMES TO SALES:**

_____

_____

_____

_____

_____

_____

_____

_____

_____

_____

**TRANSFORM SALES FROM BEING
SALESY TO ENJOYABLE!**

_____

_____

_____

_____

_____

_____

Objections are often a response to a lack of belief, lack of action, or lack of resources.

Do you experience a lack of belief in yourself? Do you lack belief that your services will work for your clients? Or do you lack commitment to your goals? Maybe you are missing something logistical which needs to take place before a transformation can happen. Check the list below to see which areas you need to work on:

- ☑ Belief in yourself
- ☐ Belief that your work will help your clients
- ☐ Commitment to take action on your goals
- ☐ Mentorship and guidance
- ☐ Accountability and support system in place

WHAT I NEED TO WORK ON:

1 REFLECT

Reflect on what you're good at and where you might need to improve

2

SET GOALS

Set goals to improve in areas
where you feel less confident

3 ACTION

Take steps towards your goals and celebrate your progress

PROSPECTING SCHEDULE

Connect with Prospects | Earn their Respect, Trust & Loyalty

MONDAY

TUESDAY

WEDNESDAY

THURSDAY

FRIDAY

SATURDAY

OVERCOMING OBJECTIONS

The next time you get frustrated by your prospect's objections, remember: anyone can sell to eager prospects. Successful real estate agents exist for the difficult customers, the ones who say, "No," "Maybe next month," and, "Yes, but …" So start overcoming objections, and stop letting them overcome you. Create your objection management document, practice your responses, then get out there and close more deals.

02

An objection can be discouraging. Mostly because it can seem like a rejection. But the truth is it is more of an opportunity to build stronger relationships and achieve greater success.

Objections from potential clients can actually be a positive sign that they are interested in working with you. It shows that they are engaged and taking the time to consider whether you're the right fit for their needs. Your response makes all the difference. This is why it is important to know how to process and handle objections.

The first step to handling objections is to view them as an opportunity rather than a roadblock. You need to remember that objections are not personal attacks on you or your service. Rather, they are a natural part of the sales process. By embracing objections and using them as an opportunity to showcase your expertise and problem-solving skills, you can turn even the most skeptical prospect into a loyal client.

Stop wondering how you can do that and listen carefully. When you're faced with an objection, never disagree or try to convince them that they're wrong. Instead, take the time to listen actively and understand the root of the concern. This will allow you to craft a thoughtful response that addresses the specific issue at hand.

Put yourself in their shoes. I bet you too object to people's offers all the time, and it is never personal. Just like you go through emotions, remember that everyone else goes through emotions too. So be kind and empathetic. Relate to their concerns and figure out how to assure them you are on their side, and only looking out for their best interest at heart. After all, that is the truth.

Now while objections may seem different on the surface, they often stem from one of these primary objections:

1 LACK OF BUDGET
They don't see the value in your service, or they simply can not justify the expense.

To address this objection, you can focus on the value and benefits that your service provides, tell and show evidence to support your claims. Show them how they will actually be saving money using you.

2 LACK OF TIME
The prospect either does not have enough time or feeling rushed to make a decision.

People often put off taking action, even when they know it's in their best interest. To address this objection, emphasize the urgency and importance of your message, and provide clear, actionable steps that your prospect can take right away.

3 LACK OF TRUST
Trust objections often stem from a lack of faith in the provider or a perceived risk associated with the sale.

Building trust takes time, and it can be hard when you're facing a skeptical prospect. Lead them to learn about you, what you do, and how you can help them. Be genuine, respectful & ethical. Use testimonials & social proof to show that you can deliver on what you promise.

4 LACK OF NEED
They don't fully understand how your offer works or don't see how it fits into their life, wants and needs.

Some prospects will tell you the service isn't a good fit for them, or give you the brush-off. You need to demonstrate that you truly understand their needs. Help them see the benefits.

The second step to handling objections is to build trust and credibility. Trust is not given, it is earned. And you can earn it by being yourself, being authentic but also diplomatic. This is where skills such as interpersonal skills, communication, leadership, conflict resolution and emotional intelligence to navigate professional interactions, come in handy.

Credibility, on the other hand, is your expertise and knowledge. The way to establish it is by using success stories, and do the little dance of show and tell.

Now that the cat is out of the box, let's talk about handling your prospects' objections. Just like you learned how to handle your own objections to pursuing your true purpose and achieving your set goals, you can learn to address and handle theirs.

Most objections arise where there's doubt, and they tango around uncertainty and fear. Fear of loss, fear of failure, fear of being duped. It's well known, doubt festers and creates insecurities, eventually leading to fear and indecisiveness, and comes full circle.

Feeling powerless, overthinking, anxiety , all result from previous negative experiences. So if your prospect's objection is that they don't think you can help them, it is most probably the residue of an unpleasant memory of a transaction that went wrong and left a bad taste in their mouths. And has absolutely nothing to do with you. You need to realize that most people are not conscious of their behavioral patterns. Mostly because they don't sit down with themselves to analyze and try to comprehend their own emotions and responses to them.

Moving on! Let's dig deeper into the origin of most objections, doubt! Doubt usually means lack of evidence. This means your prosects object, because they doubt you will make good on your promise. They need proof and assurance. But how will you provide that?

STORIES AND TESTIMONIALS

Testimonials are probably the most powerful way of overcoming objections. Mainly because they provide the evidence to proof you can do what you say you can do. But the story you tell should relate to their exact concern. Is it money, is it time, is it trust or they simply fail to see your value?

By asking the right questions, you can always get to the bottom of it. Figuring out the concern behind the objection, is already half the solution. And once you know what you're dealing with, all you need to do is come up with the right strategy and pick up the right story.

So now you know, an objection means there's something missing. And once you know what it is, you need to fill up the lack and bridge that gap. Understanding this fact and knowing how to work with it can be a valuable skill in both personal and professional aspects of life. Because objections come up in personal relationships as well, where communication breakdowns or differing perspectives can lead to misunderstandings and conflicts.

In a nutshell, when someone objects, whether it's personal or business, take the time to listen empathetically to their concerns, and understand where they are coming from. This will help you correctly identify their concern, and you will be able to provide the information and reassurance they so need to make an informed decision. Build stronger relationships and achieve greater success.

PRACTICE MAKES
PERFECT

BE
YOUR
OWN
MUSE

03

GIVE IT YOUR ALL

AND REMEMBER ...
ANYTHING WORTH HAVING TAKES TIME

How to
PRACTICE

READ THE OBJECTION TWICE. FIRST TO UNDERSTAND IT. AND SECOND TO EMPATHIZE.

TAKE A MOMENT TO IMAGINE THE PERSON WHO USES THIS OBJECTION AND TRY TO THINK OF ALL THE POSSIBLE REASONS BEHIND IT.

READ THE CLUES BELOW THE OBJECTION.

GIVE YOUR RESPONSE AND WRITE IT DOWN OR RECORD IT BEFORE GOING TO THE NEXT ONE.

TURN THE PAGE AND READ THE SUGGESTED RESPONSE. IS IT A MATCH?

YES! YOU'RE AWESOME! IF YOU THINK YOU CAME UP WITH A BETTER RESPONSE, PLEASE SHARE IT WITH US IN OUR FB COMMUNITY!

ENJOYING THIS BOOK? YOU CAN ALWAYS PRACTICE WITH A FRIEND. AND BOUNCE IDEAS OFF OF EACH OTHER. OR FIND S.O. TO PRACTICE WITH IN OUR FB COMMUNITY.

IF YOU FIND THIS BOOK HELPFUL, PLEASE GIVE IT A FIVE STAR FUN REVIEW AND SHARE WITH FRIENDS AND COLEAGUES!

MY FRIEND /RELATIVE IS AN AGENT

VERIFY INFORMATION,OFFER AN
ALTERNATIVE VALUE

PROSPECT HAS LACK OF

HOW CAN I FILL IT UP?

AweSo **ME**

"Well, that sounds great! I can appreciate your loyalty and that is a quality that I respect in people. I probably would not be able to share all my personal, and especially my financial information with a friend/relative. But maybe it will work for you! Either way, let's meet just in case to get a second opinion and see all your options."

NEVER ARGUE. EXPLAIN YOUR VALUE
AND WHY YOU'RE WORTH THEIR TIME

PROSPECT HAS LACK OF

HOW CAN I FILL IT UP?

"Sure! Who isn't? But I'm not asking you to give me anything. I'm asking you to invest in your own future. And I wouldn't be calling, if I couldn't help you."

ACKNOWLEDGE THEIR PAIN AND OFFER A SOLUTION

PROSPECT HAS LACK OF

HOW CAN I FILL IT UP?

"Please accept my apology. But the market right now is pretty fast paced and I want to make sure that you are well informed and receiving all market updates so you do not miss out on any opportunities. Would you like to meet up instead of discussing this over the phone?"

I DECIDED TO CONTINUE TO RENT FOR NOW

OFFER FINANCING REFERRALS

PROSPECT HAS LACK OF

HOW CAN I FILL IT UP?

AweSo
ME

"That's OK! But May I ask why? By the way, did you know that mortgage could be cheaper than rent. And you can build equity, & get more house. I can send you a list of lenders who would be happy to help you and qualify you for a home.

If nothing else, you owe it to yourself to at least see your options and get financial advice from an expert."

I DID NOT REGISTER ON YOUR WEBSITE!

BE UNDERSTANDING BUT ALSO DOUBLE CHECK

PROSPECT HAS LACK OF

HOW CAN I FILL IT UP?

"Oh, I see! Maybe a friend or family registered with your information. Are you thinking about buying or selling a home, or maybe you would like to invest in real estate?

Or maybe you know somebody who is?"

I CAN SELL MY HOME ON MY OWN

UNDERSTAND THEIR UNDERLYING NEEDS BASED ON THEIR OBJECTION. IT WILL HELP TO SUPPORT THE DIALOGUE AND BUILD TRUST

PROSPECT HAS LACK OF

HOW CAN I FILL IT UP?

AweSo
ME

"I understand where you're coming from. If you decide you do not want to use us, it would still be a great idea for us to connect so you could explore all your options that available to you, and all the benefits you can get. Can we meet today or tomorrow, five or six o'clock, whichever works better for you."

JUST SEND ME AN EMAIL

DON'T CUT THE CONVERSATION SHORT.
USE OPEN-ENDED FOLLOW-UP
QUESTIONS AND BUILD RAPPORT

PROSPECT HAS LACK OF

HOW CAN I FILL IT UP?

"Sure! I'd be happy to email our free guide/market updates over to you, But before I do, I would like to ask you just a couple of quick questions, so I could send you what you would be most interested in. I wouldn't want to waste your time."

*Ask qualifying questions regarding budget, timeframe, etc.

WE ALREADY WORK WITH AN AGENT

ASK OPEN-ENDED QUESTIONS, LISTEN
CAREFULLY, FIND CRACKS, SHOW
VALUE, BUILD TRUST & CREDIBILITY

PROSPECT HAS LACK OF

HOW CAN I FILL IT UP?

"That's fantastic!
But what concerns me is that
you don't have a direct line of
communication with your agent,
and you had to go through our
website to get more information
which is supposed to be already
given to you by your agent! Are
they giving you full service?
Have you actually signed an
agency agreement?"

WE ALREADY HAVE AN AGENT

ASK VERIFYING QUESTIONS, LISTEN, FIND CRACKS, SHOW & DIFFERENTIATE YOUR VALUE, BUILD TRUST & CREDIBILITY

PROSPECT HAS LACK OF

HOW CAN I FILL IT UP?

"That sounds great. Are they with (your brokerage)? Have you actually signed an agency agreement?

If you don't mind me asking, why did you choose (Agent)?"

I DON'T HAVE TIME TO TALK TO YOU RIGHT NOW

VERIFY IF IT'S REALLY A LACK OF TIME, OR IF IT'S SOMETHING ELSE, LISTEN, VALIDATE AND OFFER A SOLUTION

PROSPECT HAS LACK OF

HOW CAN I FILL IT UP?

"I completely understand. I've been busy all morning too, and this is a crazy time of year. When would be a good time to call you back?"

I'M NOT INTERESTED

EMPATHIZE, RELATE, KEEP GOING AND
SCHEDULE THE APPOINTMENT

PROSPECT HAS LACK OF

HOW CAN I FILL IT UP?

"That's all right, I hear you! In fact, most of my loyal clients told me the exact same thing and now they couldn't be happier they actually took the time to explore their options!

Would you share with me the reason why? Or what would make you interested? How about we discuss this over a cup of coffee?"

I NEED TO THINK ABOUT IT

ASK OPEN-ENDED QUESTIONS, LISTEN CAREFULLY, PIN POINT THEIR FEAR/CONCERN AND OFFER A SOLUTION

PROSPECT HAS LACK OF

HOW CAN I FILL IT UP?

"Sounds fair. Making decisions can be overwhelming. But if I may ask, what is the main thing holding you back?

What if I could help you explore all your possible options? And showed you how you could make this actually happen?

I HAVE TO DISCUSS THIS WITH MY SPOUSE

ASK OPEN-ENDED QUESTIONS, LISTEN CAREFULLY, AND OFFER A SOLUTION

PROSPECT HAS LACK OF

HOW CAN I FILL IT UP?

AweSo
ME

"Absolutely. I also discuss important decisions with my spouse. Do you think s/he will have some questions? What type of questions do you think s/he will have? You know, I believe if we get together, I could give you a better idea of what I can do for you, and address all of yours and your spouses concerns. What is a good time to meet with you and your spouse?"

I'VE SOLD MY LAST PROPERTY BY MYSELF AND DIDN'T NEED HELP

ASK OPEN-ENDED QUESTIONS, LISTEN CAREFULLY, VALIDATE AND OFFER A SOLUTION

PROSPECT HAS LACK OF

HOW CAN I FILL IT UP?

"I'm thrilled to hear that! It sounds like you know what you're doing. How are you currently marketing your property? What about vetting buyers? And scheduling showings?
I'd love to give you some professional recommendations."

I HATE YOU

NEVER TURN AN ARGUEMENT INTO A CONFLICT. IF THIS IS A DEAD-END OBJECTION, REFER TO ANOTHER AGENT

PROSPECT HAS LACK OF

HOW CAN I FILL IT UP?

"I'm sorry you feel this way about our communication. I understand, I might not be everyone's cup of tea. I could refer you to my colleague [Name] to continue the conversation. Perhaps, they'll be a better fit for you."

I DON'T THINK YOU CAN HELP ME WITH ANYTHING

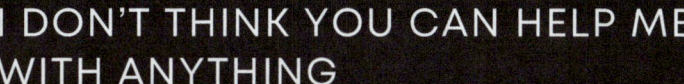

PAINT A CLEAR PICTURE OF ALL THE BENEFITS FROM WORKING WITH YOU. LEVERAGE SUCCESS STORIES

PROSPECT HAS LACK OF

HOW CAN I FILL IT UP?

AweSo
ME

"I understand, I mean if you did,
you would have called me!
But seriously, I know you get a
lot of calls, and every now and
then it makes sense to listen to
the right call, and this is it."
(Continue on with your value and
success story, and then ask
them: "Do you think you would
benefit if I could help you, too?"

I DON'T HAVE TO LISTEN TO YOU

ACKNOWLEDGE THEIR PAIN. EXPRESS
COMPASSION AND EXPLAIN YOUR VALUE

PROSPECT HAS LACK OF

HOW CAN I FILL IT UP?

"Believe me, I'm with you. But the good news is that taking just 2 minutes with me right now could change the way you look at things, and could help you save time and money, and energy. In fact, let me share briefly with you how we've helped many homeowners just like you."

I DON'T WANT TO WASTE MY TIME ON THIS CALL

VALIDATE THEIR CONCERNS, EXPLAIN THE BENEFITS.SHOW HOW YOU CAN HELP

PROSPECT HAS LACK OF

HOW CAN I FILL IT UP?

AweSo
ME

"Absolutely not! I really don't want to waste your time or mine. But let me ask you this, If I can show you how you can get your home sold faster and for top dollar, wouldn't it be worth a few minutes to find out how?"

I WILL WORK WITH YOU IF YOU LOWER YOUR COMMISSION

SHIFT THEIR FOCUS ONTO THEIR MAIN GOAL: SAVING MONEY WHILE WORKING WITH YOU

PROSPECT HAS LACK OF

HOW CAN I FILL IT UP?

"I understand your desire to save more money, & my goal is to help you do exactly that. Let me ask you this: would you want to an agent that sells your house or an agent who sells your house for the best price on the market? How are you making sure that you are paid your fair price? I want you to see me so you could trust me & know my value. Now do you want to sell your house for the best price?"

I WANT TO FIND A HOUSE BEFORE I PUT MINE ON THE MARKET

EMPHASIZE THE PROCESS OF BUYING AND SELLING A HOME AND THE CONS AND PROS

PROSPECT HAS LACK OF

HOW CAN I FILL IT UP?

AweSo
ME

"Terrific! Have you seen a home you want to put a contract on? I can help you find the perfect home. But in the mean time, let's work on getting your home sold. So that when we get your home under contract, we can put in a contract on your dream home and try to close both homes the same day. Won't that be awesome?"

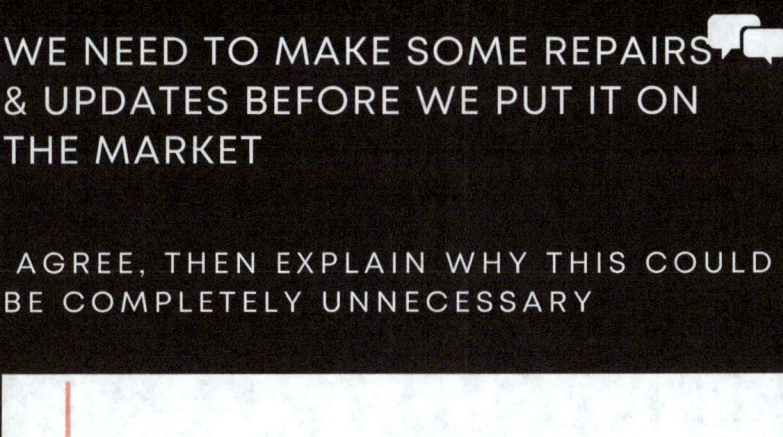

WE NEED TO MAKE SOME REPAIRS & UPDATES BEFORE WE PUT IT ON THE MARKET

AGREE, THEN EXPLAIN WHY THIS COULD BE COMPLETELY UNNECESSARY

PROSPECT HAS LACK OF

HOW CAN I FILL IT UP?

"I agree, making sure the house is up to par is important, but probably will have little effect on securing a buyer. May I ask how much you will spend on that. Because I'd hate for you to end up not making that money back on the sale. Let's check the potential and try to save you the time and money ok?"

THE PRICE YOU QUOTED US WAS LOWER THAN THE OTHER AGENT'S

VALIDATE THEIR CONCERN, EXPLAIN THE POWER OF YOUR PRICING & MARKETING STRATEY

PROSPECT HAS LACK OF

HOW CAN I FILL IT UP?

AweSo
ME

"I agree! We can certainly list at a higher price, & we can always come down in price later. But if we come out of the gate with your home overpriced, most buyers agents will write you off as non-motivated seller, which will result in the home sitting longer on the market, & a reduction might go unnoticed or signal to buyers that there's something wrong with the house."

I DON'T THINK I CAN BUY WITH MY CREDIT RIGHT NOW

VALIDATE THEIR CONCERN, EXPLAIN THE BENEFITS OF EXPLORING MORE OPTIONS

PROSPECT HAS LACK OF

HOW CAN I FILL IT UP?

AweSo
ME

"I see. But I sincerely encourage you to research your options, because there are credit repair companies that have successfully helped many clients boost their credit scores so they could get the loan they needed to purchase their dream home. I would love to connect you to a colleague of mine, who can help you explore your options and take the necessary steps in this direction."

I AM AWESOME

Got objections that were not found here? Share in our fb community for handling suggestions

⌄⌄

facebook.com/groups/awesomepeoplegroupforum

SCAN

TO JOIN OUR
AWESOME PEOPLE GROUP

AweSoME
PEOPLE GROUP

visit our website for more
AwesomePeoplegGroup.com

YOUR
SUCCESS
FORMULA

Sustainable Habits · Consistency · Positive Mindset

Beliefs · Actions · Resources · Conditions

04

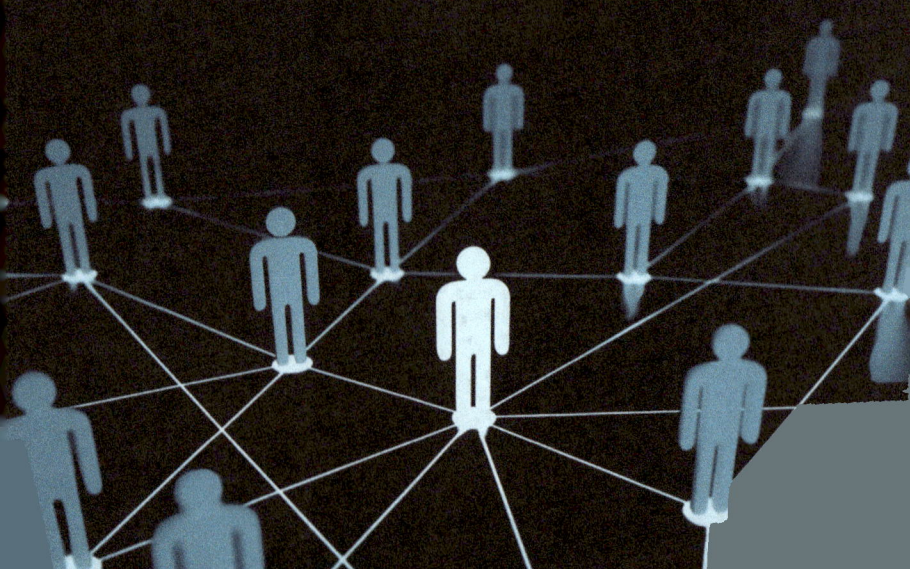

DESIRE AND DETERMINATION

Achieving success is really not a hard thing once you know what you truly desire. You need to be able, willing and ready to put in the work and commit to it. Having a positive attitude goes without saying.

Once you realize your passion, and make the decision to pursue it as your life purpose. Continue to maintain that positive energy even during tough times.

OPTIMIZING YOUR RELATIONSHIPS

The only other thing you really need is people: those who will help and support you, those who will work with you, and those who will use your services.

ACQUIRED SKILLS

Achieving any goal in life requires you to constantly grow and develop. Expand your knowledge and understanding of the ever-evolving world around you. But to do so, you need to be willing to explore new ideas, perspectives and approaches.

ACQUIRED SKILLS

Embrace change, overcome challenges, build resilience and become more flexible in your thinking and problem-solving abilities. If you desire to stay relevant, competitive and successful, you need to be able to adapt to new situations and learn new skills quickly.

Always take advantage of new opportunities that come your way.

SUPPORTIVE HABITS

Discipline. Along with drive and patience. Consistency and a strong work ethics make people more successful. But you can find out what works for you by trial and error. Then do more of what works.

Building new habits that you discover to be helpful can be a challenge. But remember, what's out of sight is out of mind, so make sure you place them always in front of you. Rewarding yourself right after will make them more attractive and easier to do.

Create

PLANNING

Decide in detail how to do something before you actually start to do it. Even though things may not always turn out as planned, having a plan in place can be helpful in keeping you on track, and further you faster in pursuing your purpose.

Some people just wing it, and it can work. As long as you have your vision clear in front of you, stay calm and collected all of the time. The truth is, everyone starts out by basically winging it, but at some point you will gain the knowledge and the experience, to know exactly what needs to be done. Because we learn from our mistakes and through trial and error. That is how we actually evolve and develop our way of life and doing things.

MY
SUCCESS FORMULA

PROSPECT'S CONCERN	MY STRATEGY	MY PROOF STORY

PROSPECT'S CONCERN	MY STRATEGY	MY PROOF STORY

www.ingramcontent.com/pod-product-compliance
Lightning Source LLC
Chambersburg PA
CBHW070121010626
45794CB00012B/951